A teen's Spirit

Changing the World Through Love and Kindness

Written By
Marci Quinn

Dedicated to A & G, my angels.

"Child of God, you were created
to create the good, the beautiful and the holy." [1]
(A Course In Miracles, T-1.VII.2:1)

The author of this book does not dispense medical advice or prescribe the use of any technique as a form of treatment for physical, emotional, or medical problems without the advice of a physician, either directly or indirectly. The intent of the author is only to offer information of a general nature to help you in your quest for emotional, physical, and spiritual well-being. In the event you use any of the information in this book for yourself, the author assumes no responsibility for your actions.
Because of the dynamic nature of the Internet, any web addresses or links in this book may have been changed since publication and may no longer be valid.

For more information, email thekindkraftproject@gmail.com or visit www.TheKindKraftProject.com.

First Edition
Paperback ISBN: 978-1-7351863-0-6
E-book ISBN: 978-1-7351863-1-3

A Teen's Spirit

Changing the World Through Love and Kindness

Written By
Marci Quinn

Introduction

When I was at a pivotal point in my life around the age of 14, I had two paths to choose from. I could have chosen to stay the path of my childhood innocence or veer off into more self-defeating behaviors and thought patterns. In choosing the latter, it took a couple decades of mistakes and struggling to understand how to be happy and at peace. While I don't regret my past because it brought me to where I am today, I know that there are ways to learn about life through love instead of pain.

The principles illustrated in this book can help show the path to a truly purposeful life. One that is full of joy and miracles. My hope is that it can also provide hope and inspiration for the next generation—and give some clarity about how we can use our connection to our Higher Power, or God, to give us the strength and answers we need to live a life of joy.

I make mention of God throughout parts of this book. The word "God" can mean anything that represents a higher power to you (the universe, the Source, Divine Energy etc.). My mention of God does not align with any religion—the word is used more as a concept of a divine force that is in play in the universe.

I also list song lyrics and their artists throughout this book as well as inspirational quotes from prominent and impactful people. I encourage you to listen to them, watch the videos of each online or simply learn more about the speaker quoted. I personally find each song and quotation to be uplifting and inspiring.

I hope you find meaning within this book and with each page, develop a newfound understanding of the world and of yourself.

Our Job on Earth

Do you ever wonder what the purpose of life is? What are we doing here on Earth? Think of living on this planet as being enrolled in "Earth School" [2], a term from the self-help book Seat of the Soul by Gary Zukav. We are here on Earth to learn how to be kind and compassionate to everyone, including ourselves. No matter what situation we are faced with, it is our job to learn how to face it in a way that carries out God's will, which is what God wants us to do with ourselves every moment of every day. God's will is always love, compassion, and forgiveness for everyone. God loves all of us no matter what. He forgives us no matter what. He created each and every one of us and loves all of us unconditionally.

It may seem like the most important tasks in our lives are things such as getting a good grade on a test, scoring the winning goal in a soccer game or getting into a good college. While it is important to do our best at each task throughout the day, our real job is to express love and compassion while performing these everyday tasks. Let's say you got an A on a test, but in doing so you cheated by copying your classmate's answer. So, while you did get an A, it was not achieved in the right way. While it is important to make sure our lives are going in a positive direction, the real job lies in *how* we do that to the best of our ability.

God Will Guide You in the Right Direction

How do you know what the right thing to do is? Well, inside your heart, there is a feeling called your intuition. That feeling is God speaking to you, guiding you in the right direction, hence the term "God's Will." He will always guide you to thinking and doing things that are aligned with the best version of yourself. If you stay in faith that God's will can lead you to happiness and joy, you can find more peace and less worry in your life. If we try to do the right thing throughout our lifetime, our hearts will be filled with love and peace. Sometimes, however, you will find that doing the right thing is not the easy choice. It is at this point where it's important to have faith that doing the right thing, even though it doesn't seem easy, will bring positive results to your life.

Everything that happens to us is for our greater good—it is God teaching us lessons that we need to learn to become all-loving beings. If something happens to you that you perceive as not good at that moment, try to look at it from a different perspective to see how in fact, it is serving your greater good. For example, maybe you got your class assignment for the new school year and learned that none of your friends will be in your class this year. You might feel sad and scared that you will have no friends in your class and assume that the year will not be good. Once you get into your classroom—and as the days go on—you meet new friends that you find you have a lot in common with and enjoy being around. Furthermore, you get to see your old friends at lunch and during after school activities every day, too. So, instead of looking at this situation as negative, look at it as open for possibility.

The same can be said for how we choose to react in certain situations. If you are at school and see a child being made fun of, how does that make you feel? Would you feel better about yourself if you joined in or if you stood up for what was right and helped your peer? Your heart tells you that this child needs a friend, and you are that friend. When I was in high school, there was a girl in the grade below me, who was called names by other students. They thought poorly of her, voiced these negative comments and left the girl alone to cry. My heart broke for her because I had experienced a similar feeling of upset that same year. I knew it was my job to help her feel better. As everyone left the lunchroom, I stayed behind and talked to her and let her know that she was not what they said she was. She gave me a hug and thanked me. This was a defining moment in my life where I felt what it was like to stand up for what I believed was right.

If you see a homeless person on the street asking for spare change, would you feel better giving them some money or just walking by them and doing nothing? It is easier to rationalize in your head why you shouldn't give them any attention or money or food. Maybe you think that there are so many homeless people that helping one in such a small way wouldn't do any good. Or maybe you don't believe that they are truly homeless or would use your contribution to buy alcohol or cigarettes. While we cannot know these things, what we do know is that in that moment, giving that person a dollar means much more to them than you would ever know. You are demonstrating selflessness, kindness, and compassion to that person with one simple act. Their heart feels the love from you, and you will feel good in your heart as well. You may also inspire others who witness your act of kindness to act as well, creating a ripple effect of charity and basic human decency.

I am in New York City often and I try to make a habit of bringing granola bars or easily portable fruit to give to anyone who seems in need of food. One time, I packed a small bag of food, toiletries, socks, some money etc., and was actively looking for someone to give it to but I couldn't find the right person for this bag. I stopped looking, and that is when a woman came up to me on the subway and asked for some food. I knew she was the one who needed this. She took it and said, "God Bless you," took a seat and started going through the bag in delight. This brought more joy to me that day than anything else. It turned a frequent trip to Manhattan into a day I will never forget.

"Darkness cannot drive out darkness; only light can do that. Hate cannot drive out hate; only love can do that."

- Martin Luther King, Jr. [3]

Photo by Sandy Burr Photography (SandyBurrPhotograhy.com)

Activity: Make A Peace Flag

Peace Flags provide a way for you to express your hopes and dreams for a better, more peaceful world. *(Peace Flags were inspired by Tibetan Prayer flags, which are decorated with images of peace, kindness, and love; Tibetans believe these messages are sent around the world on the wind.)* The flags symbolize that we are all connected as One, and that we all want the same things in life: love, peace, and joy.

To order your own Peace Flag kit,
you can visit *www.thepeaceflagproject.org*

Materials Needed:
5 pieces of cotton fabric approximately 9" x 9"" each,
5 different colors of fabric in light shades.

Permanent markers or acrylic paint markers in a variety of colors
1 piece of twine, about 7 feet long
Glue
Cardstock or Cardboard
Clothespins

• *Tape your fabric to a surface so it stays in place, making sure to protect any surface from marker. It's good to use cardstock or cardboard to protect your surface. Do the same for each of the five flags.*

• *Draw words and/or images of peace and love on each flag that you want to send out the world. Leave about an inch on top of the flag to fold over the twine you'll use to hang the flags.*

• *Lay out the piece of twine on the floor and arrange the five completed flags upside down. Leave a couple inches between each flag and about a foot on each end.*

• *Apply a thin line of glue half an inch from the top of the flag and fold the fabric over. Attach the clothespins to help keep it in place until it dries, or just press firmly for a minute or so.*

• *Hang your peace flag outside so the wind can take the messages around the world. Or hang in your house as a reminder of peace and love in the world.*

– Martin Luther King, Jr. –
Nobel Peace Prize Winner (1964)

Martin Luther King Jr. was a Baptist minister and civil rights activist in the 1950s and 1960s. As a black American, his mission was to have all men and women treated equally regardless of their race. He would only use non-violent means such as peaceful protests & transportation bans to inspire change.

By using his platform as a minister, he gave motivational speeches to encourage others to join in for the sake of peace and equality. To him, standing up for what he believed in no matter what, was of the utmost importance in his life. His life and legacy are honored every year on Martin Luther King Jr. Day near his birthday in January.

"The time is always right to do what is right."
– Martin Luther King, Jr.[4]

We Are All One

We must realize that we are all connected—if you spread kindness to others, kindness will be returned to you. If you withhold kindness, expect the same in return. This is the law of cause and effect. Whatever you put out into the world comes back to you. God created us all from his love, and so it is that we are all connected by this energy of love.

Expressing any gesture of love or kindness to someone else can affect more than just you and that other person. If other witness acts of kindness, they could be more likely to act kindly themselves. If someone was just helped by a stranger, they could be more likely to help the next person in need. There is a ripple effect of kindness that we cannot always see, but trust that it does happen.

The next time you face an issue where you can react negatively *(with fear)* or positively *(with love)*, you can practice positivity and see what happens. Let's say you don't get picked to be on the team you wanted to be on; you can either accept it and try your best to win the game or you can get angry and choose to not play, ruining the game for your teammates and ultimately, yourself. But what if you did play, your team ended up winning and you made a new friend at the same time? You also may have inspired others to be a team player as well. If you choose not to play, you would have missed out on these possibilities.

Activity: Make A Kokedama Plant

A kokedama plant or "moss ball," is a Japanese style of planting that uses moss to cover the soil of an ornamental plant. It can be hung by string in your window or placed in a shallow decorative bowl.

According to Japan's native religion of Shinto, "individuals and nature, past and present, the human and the divine, are all as one," [5] (May Carroll, www.themossandgreen.com).

There is a spirit of peace and oneness behind the act of creating the Kokedama, which emphasizes staying in the present moment and connecting with nature. In this connection with nature, creating a kokedama plant can help people experience love and joy, which is passed on through the kokedama plant to others.

Materials Needed:

A small plant of your choice (a small jade or lady fern are good choices)
Peat moss, Bonsai soil, and Akadama soil 6:2:2 ratio
Sphagnum moss or fresh garden moss
Waxed string or twine
Scissors
Large bowl
Water

- Mix the Peat moss, Bonsai soil, and Akadama soil at a 6:2:2 ratio in a large bowl with some water.

- Remove plant from container and carefully remove as much soil from around the roots as you can.

- Sculpt a ball of the soil mix in your hands, a bit larger than a baseball, pressing out any extra water.

- Split the ball of soil in half and place the roots of the plant into the ball, using your hands to firmly sculpt the soil ball around the plant.

- Lay the moss flat on your surface and place the soil ball in the center. Wrap the moss around the soil ball, so all parts come together at the base of the plant. Wrap a piece of string or twine around the top of the moss ball and tie it together.

- Wrap an additional piece of twine or string around the moss ball to help keep it together.

- Place your kokedama in a shallow dish or tie strings around the plant to hang it from a hook.

- Mist the moss ball with water. Each week soak the moss ball in a bowl of room temperature water for about 15 minutes. Once the soil is saturated, gently wring out excess water and return it to its dish after it has dried.

We Are All Equal

We all might seem different on the outside—skin color, body type, style, personality, etc., but God created us all equally. We are all God's children born from the same source—love. We all want the same things—peace, joy, and happiness. It might be hard to see this sometimes, especially when you see somebody acting mean or hurtful. However, when someone is acting this way, it means they feel bad about themselves inside, and what they really need is love from others.

The next time you see someone having a hard time, help them out. We can't assume we know what they are going through at that moment.

Maybe they just had an argument with their parents, or they don't feel well physically or mentally. You can also make an effort to be kind to a bully; maybe that's exactly what they need to change their heart. If you notice someone who looks sad, that's your opportunity to help cheer them up. You may not know their story, but you can help lighten their burden. In doing so, you will be carrying out God's will, or His mission for you in that moment. And in carrying out God's will, happiness is sure to follow.

Cyndi Lauper - True Colors [6]

You with the sad eyes
Don't be discouraged
Oh I realize
It's hard to take courage
In a world full of people
You can lose sight of it all
And the darkness inside you
Can make you feel so small

But I see your true colors
Shining through
I see your true colors
And that's why I love you
So don't be afraid to let them show
Your true colors
True colors are beautiful
Like a rainbow

Show me a smile then
Don't be unhappy
Can't remember when
I last saw you laughing
If this world makes you crazy
And you've taken all you can bear
You call me up
Because you know I'll be there

And I'll see your true colors
Shining through
I see your true colors
And that's why I love you
So don't be afraid to let them show
Your true colors
True colors are beautiful
Like a rainbow

If this world makes you crazy
You've taken all you can bear
You call me up
Because you know I'll be there

And I'll see your true colors
Shining through
I see your true colors
And that's why I love you
So don't be afraid to let them show
Your true colors
True colors

True colors are shining through
I see your true colors
And that's why I love you
So don't be afraid to let them show
Your true colors
True colors are beautiful
Like a rainbow

– Youth Activism –

A new generation of youth activists are emerging in this country and around the world. The issues our planet and humanity face have reached a point in which drastic change is necessary and many of today's youth are heeding the call to service. Issues such as climate change, homelessness and hunger, animal cruelty, violence in schools and more have become all too common. It's up to all of us to do our part to make the world a better place.

Today's youth are stepping up to the plate and doing what they can to make the world a better place. Young entrepreneurs are starting non-profits to help people and animals in need. Teenagers are speaking out about the urgency for all of us to do all we can to reverse the devastating effects of climate change. Greta Thunberg is a 17-year-old Swedish environmental activist, who uses her voice to speak about the effects that climate change is having on our planet.

She has pioneered the way for young activists to speak up about causes that are important to them. Her passion and dedication to this cause not only impacts and inspires the youth, but older generations as well.

Is there a cause that you would like to learn more about? Research an issue that is interesting or relevant to you and try to think of small ways that you can help. Brainstorm with your friends and your family. Maybe you can organize a group of like-minded people to help bring awareness and change to your issue? Or maybe you can start by simply educating those close to you about the issue and why you are so passionate about it.

> *"It takes a strong woman to stand up for herself...*
> *it takes a stronger woman to stand up for everyone else."*
> *- (Anonymous, 2019)*

Mistakes and Forgiveness

We all are human and that means we have faults. If you know you made a mistake and you want to feel better inside, first acknowledge that you made the error to God and yourself. Apologize if possible, to whoever may have been affected by your mistake. God forgives you for he knows forgiveness is the path to love. The same goes for when others make mistakes. It is important to forgive others, as we would wish to be forgiven for our own wrongdoings. It is not our job to judge or criticize others or to prove that we are right—people will learn on their own through the laws of cause and effect, also known as karma. Karma says that whatever we give, we receive back. So, if we give love and forgiveness, that we shall receive in return. If we give anger, resentment and hatred, that sentiment will also come back to us in some way. People will experience their own consequences naturally. It is simply our job to forgive and to love. And in forgiving others, it helps us to forgive ourselves, therefore, lightening our own hearts. I truly believe that forgiveness of ourselves and others is the key to happiness and peace.

> "The weak can never forgive. Forgiveness
> is the attribute of the strong."
> -Mahatma Gandhi

Think about forgiveness like this: If you got upset with your younger brother or sister for ruining your favorite video game or electronic device, and you in turn, got angry, yelled at them, and made them cry, I'm sure you would feel bad about what you did in your heart. Maybe not in that moment, as you acted emotionally, but after you have cooled down. You might come to feel guilty or ashamed. Those negative feelings are God subtly teaching you a lesson in love. He is teaching you to not act from a place of anger, but instead to handle it in a more peaceful way. What good would it be if someone else got mad at you and yelled at you for what you said in anger on top of the bad feelings of guilt and shame you are already experiencing? It would be more helpful if someone was there for you to help fix what went wrong in a kind way. You already learned your lesson when you felt remorseful so love from others is the logical next step.

> "Each morning we are born again.
> What we do today is what matters most."
> - Buddha

– Don Miguel Ruiz –
The Four Agreements

Don Miguel Ruiz is a Mexican spiritual leader, who uses ancient Toltec wisdom to guide people to a life of peace and happiness through his insights about how to live our most purposeful life. He has summarized his thoughts into these "four agreements," that are simple, yet very powerful in changing our perspective on how we choose to live our lives.

The Four Agreements[7]

1.
Be impeccable with your word.

Speak with integrity. Say only what you mean. Avoid using the word to speak against yourself or to gossip about others.
Use the power of your word in the direction of truth and love.

2.
Don't take anything personally.

Nothing others do is because of you.
What others say and do is a projection of their own reality, their own dream. When you are immune to the opinions and actions of others, you won't be the victim of needless suffering.

3.
Don't make assumptions.

Find the courage to ask questions and to express what you really want. Communicate with others as clearly as you can to avoid misunderstandings, sadness, and drama.
With just this one agreement, you can completely transform your life.

4.
Always do your best.

Your best is going to change from moment to moment;
it will be different when you are healthy as opposed to sick.
Under any circumstance, simply do your best, and you will avoid self-judgment, self-abuse, and regret.

Prayer & Meditation

If you ever feel lonely, sad, angry, or scared, try talking to God through prayer and ask him to show you the way back to love. Be careful to listen and He will speak to you through your heart. Praying is our way to communicate with God and our job is to pay attention to His answer. Maybe you asked God to help show you the way to do better in school. Then, you learn a few days later that new neighbors are moving in and the new boy that moved in is a tutor for his part-time job. This is a sign from God that perhaps he can help you do better in school.

Here is an example of a prayer you can say in the morning:

Dear God,
"Where would You have me go?
What would You have me do?
What would You have me say, and to whom?"

- Daily prayer from A Course in Miracles [8]

While prayer is our way to talk to God, meditation is a way to listen to what He says. There are many ways to meditate but all it requires is finding a peaceful space where you are free from most distractions and noise. Sit upright with your eyes closed in a comfortable spot. Focus on your breath as you breathe normally. When your mind has wandered off to thoughts, refocus your attention on your breath. Any amount of time in meditation is beneficial. Start off at 2-3 minutes and then you can work your way up to 15-20 minutes at a time.

Additionally, you can also do a 'moving meditation' in which you take a walk free of any distractions, and just pay attention to the world around you. If you are in nature, you can take in all of the beauty that surrounds you - the swaying leaves on the trees, the birds singing, the small animals playing, the sound of the water, or the feeling of the breeze or the rain. There is nothing better than a walk in nature to recharge and inspire us.

Activity: Create a Peace Garden

A peace garden is a space you create outdoors to connect with nature and yourself. It's a place where you can be free of distractions. You can read a book, say a prayer, meditate, sketch a drawing, talk with friends, catch some sunshine, do some yoga stretches, think about things that are important to you and what good you can do that day.

If you have access to any outdoor space in your yard, find a small section that you can use. If you don't have outdoor space, you can create a small peace nook in your house or bedroom. The possibilities to set up this space are endless and are all up to you. In this area, you can:

- *Decorate the area by painting kindness rocks or ceramic tiles with words and images of love and peace.*

- *Plant some flowers that you love, or ones that have a calming effect such as lavender, chrysanthemums or wildflowers.*

- *Bring in a small bench, cushion or blanket you can sit on to make the space comfortable.*

- *Hang your peace flags in this area.*

- *Bury a small time capsule with symbols and messages of love and hope.*

Miracles Happen Everyday

Have you ever experienced a miracle?

According to A Course in Miracles, a miracle is a change in how you perceive a situation from a fearful perspective to a loving one.[9] (Marianne Williamson, A Return to Love). Perhaps there is a student in your grade who you just don't get along with and have seemingly nothing in common with. This person bothers you and has even been unkind to you in the past. Then one day, you find out that this student recently lost a parent and was having a really hard time coping with it. Suddenly, you have a change of heart and see this person from a different perspective. You realize that you want to extend kindness and compassion to them instead of judging them and thinking negative thoughts about them. You might even end up as friends with this person as a result of your change of heart and perspective. This was a change from a fear-based perspective (judging, dislike), to a love-based perspective (acceptance and empathy). A miracle!

You have the power to experience miracles every day. All you need to do is make the choice to look at all people, all problems, and all situations with love. When we default to fearful responses to what we perceive as 'bad' situations, we are subconsciously blocking ourselves from receiving a miracle. This is where faith comes in. Faith is belief that your higher power is at work, always in our best interest. We must have faith that this situation is happening to us for a reason that is for our greatest good and our greatest happiness. It is teaching us a lesson we came to Earth to learn. With patience and dedication to doing the right thing no matter what, you will experience your life change in unexpectedly amazing ways.

"There are two ways to live: you can live as if nothing is a miracle;
you can live as if everything is a miracle."
- Albert Einstein

Activity: Yoga

Yoga is a wonderful activity with countless benefits including stress reduction and relaxation, increased muscle strength and flexibility, and improved mood. A faster paced vinyasa flow set to some music is a good choice.

If you can't make it to a class, try these postures at home, or you can find countless videos online that you can do at home.

I always feel like a better version of myself after a good yoga class!

Free Will

You are always in the path of love and protection so long as you trust in God to guide your way. But you have choices, free will, every moment of the day. Each of your choices has an effect, which teaches you a lesson. We can learn our lessons through love or through pain. When we act on our free will and make decisions that will only benefit ourselves, our lessons will likely be learned through pain. When we act according to God's will, peace and joy will follow.

If we rescue a hurt puppy and nurse it back to health, we feel love and joy in our hearts. If we choose to not help the puppy, our heart will feel upset. If we join in and make fun of another person because they are different from us, we feel guilt and sadness within ourselves. But if we help that person feel better and choose not to join in, we would feel much different.

Those negative feelings are consequences of choosing to not follow our heart, or God's will. They don't make us feel good; therefore, we learn not to behave that way again. When in doubt of how to behave in any situation, always choose kindness, no matter what. That is the way of God, and if you choose to follow His path and His will, only love, joy, and peace will follow. Our choices determine our happiness, so you are in control of your own happiness.

When all of God's children choose God's will, there will be heaven on Earth. God's will is always unconditional Love and Forgiveness.

Love for everyone +
Forgiveness of everyone for everything
= Heaven on Earth

33

Everyone is Special

God created each of us with a special gift. It is our job to share this gift. Your special gift is something inside of you that will help make the world a better place. Ask yourself, what are your gifts (special talents, skills, or character traits) and how can you use them to make the world a better place?

Your gifts can come in many forms:

Artist
Create artwork that inspires others and shows beauty.

Singer
Sing songs of love and hope or volunteer at a nursing home to sing to the sick and elderly. Invite your friends to join you.

Loves children
If you love being around children, get a summer job at a children's camp or volunteer at a local children's hospital. Teach children kindness.

Good with math/science
Help solve complex environmental issues through science or join the math or science club at school. Tutor other students who might be struggling in this area.

Creative writer
Write stories of love and hope and overcoming adversity. Consider self-publishing your own book on a subject you care deeply about or are interested in. Or, write a letter to the editor of your local newspaper about an issue you feel needs to change.

Avid reader
Start a book club with your friends and invite others to join. You can even focus on positive, uplifting and inspiring books.

Athlete
Inspire others with your character, demonstrate good sportsmanship, and teach children what teamwork means.

Animal lover
Volunteer at an animal shelter or arrange a fundraiser and donate money to animal shelters or hospitals. If you are able, rescue a dog or cat.

Nature enthusiast
Help preserve the Earth and spread the message of environmentalism or arrange a community trash pickup in your town or neighborhood.

Fashionista
Strive to design clothes with sustainable materials and messages of love or take a fashion design class.

Gardener
Plant an organic vegetable garden, donate veggies to a food bank or join the Environmental Club at your school.

Organizer
Put together a fundraiser for a charity that is important to you or help others carry out their big ideas with your attention to detail. You can also inspire others to donate items they don't need and to keep a tidy, organized house.

Big idea thinker
Think about big ways to make a positive impact on the world.

Friendly
Smile and say kind greetings to people you meet. Go out of your way to include people that seem lonely.

Connecter
Help connect friends of yours with other people you know who have similar interests. You can also start a young adult activist group in your community.

If you are having a hard time identifying your special gifts, you can ask your friends or your parents what they think is special about you. Or, think about what activity or task you do during the day that brings you happiness. What makes your heart feel warm? Once you know where you shine, it's time to put it to good use.

"Your purpose in life is to find your purpose and give your whole heart and soul to it." - Buddha

- Celebrity Activism -

These days, a lot of celebrities are aligning with social causes that are important to them. Being a celebrity gives each of them a large audience to speak to in order to inspire change. Here are just a handful of examples of celebrities who have started their own foundations to help make the world a better place.

Jennifer Lopez -
This singer and actress founded The Lopez Family Foundation. "The Lopez Family Foundation is a global non-profit organization dedicated to improving the health and well-being of women and children and increasing the medical care available to them."
(The Lopez Family Foundation, Homepage,
http://www.lopezfamilyfoundation.org/ Last visited May 19, 2020).

Miley Cyrus -
This singer founded The Happy Hippie. "Our mission is to rally young people to fight injustice facing homeless youth, LGBTQ youth and other vulnerable populations."
(The Happy Hippie, Homepage, www.happyhippies.org,
last visited May 19, 2020)

John Mayer -
This singer founded The Heart and Armor Foundation. "The Heart and Armor Foundation aims to protect the health of veterans, and to connect civilians to the experience of military service members." (The Heart and Armor Foundation for Veterans Health, Homepage,
https://www.heartandarmor.org/, last visited May 25, 2020)

Bode Miller -
This Olympic skier founded The Turtle Ridge Foundation.
"The Foundation seeks to provide a philanthropic platform in the community, support youth & adaptive sports programs and to offer the opportunity for our disabled community and young people to participate in a variety of sports and recreational activities that would not be available to them without our help."

(The Turtle Ridge Foundation, Our Mission, *http://www. turtleridgefoundation.org/about-turtle-ridge-foundation/what-we-do*, last visited May 19, 2020)

Drew Brees -
This NFL quarterback founded The Brees Dream Foundation. This foundation focuses on "improving the quality of life for cancer patients, and providing care, education and opportunities for children and families in need."
(The Brees Dream Foundation, Homepage, *http://drewbrees.com/*, last visited May 25, 2020)

Leonardo DiCaprio -
This actor started The Leonardo DiCaprio Foundation in 1998. "We support projects around the world that build climate resiliency, protect vulnerable wildlife, and restore balance to threatened ecosystems and communities." This foundation is now in partnership with Earth Alliance which is "dedicated to urgently addressing climate change and environmental threats to life on Earth."(The Leonardo DiCaprio Foundation, Homepage, *https://www.leonardodicaprio.org/*, last visited May 21, 2020)

Lady Gaga-
This Grammy award winning artist co-founded the Born This Way Foundation. "Born This Way Foundation was founded in 2012 with the goal of creating a kinder and braver world."
(Born This Way Foundation, Our Mission, https://bornthisway. foundation/our-mission/, last visited May 22, 2020). They aim to "empower young people to support each other in times of need or crisis."
(Born This Way Foundation, Homepage, *https://bornthisway.foundation/*, last visited May 3, 2020).

Pink - A Million Dreams

I close my eyes and I can see
A world that's waiting up for me
That I call my own
Through the dark, through the door
Through where no one's been before
But it feels like home

They can say, they can say it all sounds crazy
They can say, they can say I've lost my mind
I don't care, I don't care, so call me crazy
We can live in a world that we design

'Cause every night I lie in bed
The brightest colors fill my head
A million dreams are keeping me awake
I think of what the world could be
A vision of the one I see
A million dreams is all it's gonna take
A million dreams for the world we're gonna make

There's a house we can build
Every room inside is filled
With things from far away
The special things I compile
Each one there to make you smile
On a rainy day

They can say, they can say it all sounds crazy
They can say, they can say we've lost our minds
I don't care, I don't care if they call us crazy
Run away to a world that we design

Every night I lie in bed
The brightest colors fill my head
A million dreams are keeping me awake
I think of what the world could be
A vision of the one I see
A million dreams is all it's gonna take
A million dreams for the world we're gonna make

However big, however small
Let me be part of it all
Share your dreams with me
You may be right, you may be wrong
But say that you'll bring me along
To the world you see
To the world I close my eyes to see
I close my eyes to see

Every night I lie in bed
The brightest colors fill my head
A million dreams are keeping me awake
A million dreams, a million dreams
I think of what the world could be
A vision of the one I see
A million dreams is all it's gonna take
A million dreams for the world we're gonna make

Take Action: Care More

We all do our best to care about our family, our friends and practice self-care within ourselves. But this is not enough in the world we live in today. We need to care more about the world outside of our own lives. Issues such as childhood hunger; violence in our schools, homes, and on the streets; and catastrophic weather events as a result of climate change are not going to change if we don't all change on a larger scale. We need to act on issues we know in our hearts need to change. It is our moral responsibility to help make a positive change now. Our small, sustained acts of kindness can change the lives of others and will also inspire others to act, creating a ripple effect.

Here are some simple actions you can take to make the world a better place:

- *If you have old clothes, books, household and baby items, food that are lying idle in your home, donate them to those in need in your community. Ask your friends and family if they have anything to donate that you can take to the needy.*

- *Recycle everything you can. If you see trash on the sidewalk, pick it up and throw it out. Organize a neighborhood trash pick-up day.*

- *Pack a small bag of granola bars, money, clean socks, toothbrush/ toothpaste/floss, essentials, and bring it into the city on your next trip to give to someone who is homeless.*

- *Offer to walk a sick or elderly neighbor's dog, rake or shovel their yard, or even just ask them how they are doing.*

- *Write a letter to your grandparents or give them a call to say hello.*

- *Bake cookies for the local fire or police department. Write a note to thank them for all they do for your community.*

- *Be a tree foster parent! Search your yard near trees and flowerbeds to find young saplings growing in the ground. Transplant them carefully with their roots into flower pots with soil. Let your sapling grow until it's big enough to transplant in your yard or donate them to the community.*

- *Eat vegan once a week. The environment and animals will thank you.*

- *Leave places cleaner than when you got there. So, clean up after yourself and pick something else you can tidy up as well. You might just save the life of an animal.*

- *Adopt an animal as a birthday or holiday gift. Check out the Adopt section at Defenders of Wildlife: https://defenders.org/*

- *Plant an organic garden. If you have extra vegetables that you won't use, give them to your neighbors or the local food bank.*

- *Create a vision board with images and words that inspire you.*

- *Volunteer at a soup kitchen to help feed those in need, or as a dogwalker at a local animal shelter.*

- *Commit a random act of kindness every day.*

- *Pray for the Earth, for the homeless, and for the sick.*

- *For the animals sake, consider avoiding zoos and aquariums. Instead, visit animal sanctuaries, go on a whale watch, safari, or just enjoy animals in nature. (http://woodstocksanctuary.org/, https://www.farmsanctuary.org/)*

- *The Obama Foundation was created by former President Barack Obama and his wife, Michelle "to inspire, empower, and connect people to change their world." (The Obama Foundation, Our Mission, www.Obama.org (last visited May 17, 2020). Visit www.Obama.org for inspiration and ways you can help make a difference in the world.*

You have the power to change the world with your unique and special gifts—it's time to put them to use for good. This is our only job here on Earth—to love all and spread kindness to all, no matter what.

"Be the change that you wish to see in the world."
— *Mahatma Gandhi*

International Day of Peace

Every year on September 21, the United Nations invites the world to celebrate International Day of Peace. This is "a day devoted to strengthening the ideals of peace, through observing 24 hours of non-violence and cease-fire."
(United Nations, Observances,
https://www.un.org/en/observances/international-day-peace,
(last visited May 2, 2020).

This is a perfect day for all of humanity to commit to spreading peace in their communities, in their homes and in their hearts. Take note of this date and give some thought to what you can do to help make the world a better place on this day and all the days that follow.

Every September, Rhode Island celebrates the United Nations International Day of Peace with a Month of Peace, culminating with PeaceFest on 9/21. This festival in Providence, RI features peace themed activities for children, performances, storytellers, exhibits, awards and a peace walk. These festivals have been organized by The Peace Flag Project.[11] (The Peace Flag Project, *www.thepeaceflagproject.org*)

Search your area to see if your area has a similar celebration or if your city or town is one of the 'Cities for Peace' (http://www. internationalcitiesofpeace.org/cities-listing/). If not, create your own Peace themed activities with your friends! This website gives a lot of wonderful ideas for kids to learn more about peace such as signing the Peace Pledge or committing to The Great Kindness Challenge. (*https://kidsforpeaceglobal.org/*).

Gratitude

Sometimes it's easy to only focus on what you want and what you feel you don't have, but instead, try being grateful for everything that you do have. This outlook will lead to positive thoughts and happiness. If you only focus on what you want, your mind will likely be full of negative thoughts. Remember, staying positive opens us up to receiving more.

We can all find countless things for which to be grateful. First and foremost, you are a child of God, and are always under his loving care and guidance. You have air to breath, clothes on your back, and food to nourish you. You have friends and family. You have nature, sunlight, and freedom.

One way to practice gratitude is to make a gratitude jar. Each day, when your family has a moment together, everyone can write down on a piece of paper one thing that they are grateful for that day. Feel free to decorate the jar however you like. The jar will eventually be filled with thoughts of gratitude. Once it's full, you and your family can read them aloud to remind everyone how blessed you really are.

You can also start a gratitude journal. Each morning or night write down three things that you are grateful for. Try not to repeat items. You might notice how many things there are in life to be grateful for. Each day brings more blessings and the more you focus on your blessings, the more blessings you will receive.

– Costa Rica, Pura Vida –

Pura Vida means "pure life" or "simple life." Pura Vida is not only the way Costa Ricans greet each other and say goodbye, but it's a way of life. This term captures the spirit of this country by celebrating the beauty in all its people and the beauty of the land. Costa Ricans are thankful for what they have and try not to focus on what they don't have. They keep life simple by enjoying fresh food, spending a lot of time outdoors, and bonding with friends and family. It's no wonder Costa Rica is the home of some of the happiest and longest living humans on the planet (Buettner, Dan. The Blue Zones, https://www.bluezones.com/2018/05/why-is-costa-rica-one-of-the-happiest-healthiest-places-on-earth/, (last visited May 3, 2020).

How can we live this 'simple, pure life' ourselves?

- *Make time spent with your family and friends a priority. Sunday dinners together can be a new family tradition. You can even invite extended family members or friends to this special meal.*

- *Focus on a whole foods, plant-based diet filled with fresh vegetables & fruits, beans, nuts, seeds and whole grains. Go to a farmers market and see what's in season in your area.*

- *Choose to spend time with friends who are supportive and inspiring to you.*

- *Make exercise a part of your daily lifestyle. Evening walks with your family, weekend morning yoga class with friends, planting a spring garden, walking your dog, etc.*

Being Conscious

Being conscious means being aware of ourselves and the impact we have on the world around us. Every choice we make has an impact, or an effect. One area where everyone has a choice is where we spend our money. There are more and more "conscious" companies being started these days.

These companies care about the ingredients they use, the impact they have on the environment, and the people who make their products. They also tend to give back a portion of their profits to charitable causes. It makes sense to try to purchase products and services from companies who care. The more we spend our money with conscious corporations who we believe demonstrates and reflects our own moral values, the more they will grow and prosper. Consider buying gifts for family and friends from companies that care and give back to humanity.

Here are just a few companies who give back:

- **Bombas socks:**
  For each pair of socks purchased, one pair is donated to those in need. (www.Bombas.com)[12]

- **Toms Shoes:**
  One of the original companies with a mission to donate one pair of shoes for every pair purchased. (www.toms.com)[13]

- **The Kind Kraft Project:**
  This company that provides classes for kids and teens on love, peace, spirituality, and social activism gives back by helping the homeless. (www.thekindkraftproject.com)[14]

- **FEED:**
A company that sells clothing, bags and accessories. Each item you buy provides a certain amount of school meals provided to children in need, through the brand's nonprofit partners. (www.feedprojects.com)[15]

- **Skylar:**
An eco-friendly fragrance and body care company. It donates a portion of proceeds to Step Up, "a non-profit organization that provides mentorship for underprivileged high school girls across the country." (www.skylar.com)[16]

- **Tentree:**
This eco-conscious apparel company plants 10 trees for each item purchased. (www.tentree.ca) [17]

We also need to give thought to what types of food we choose to eat. All foods are either made from plants or animals. Fruits, vegetables, nuts, seeds, lentils, beans, etc., are made from plants and milk, meat, cheese, and seafood are made from animals. Although it is a lifestyle choice, when choosing to eat animal-based products, extra thought and consideration needs to be given.

Consider the fact that animals are voiceless, defenseless creatures that rely on humans to protect them. If animal products are something that you choose to consume, consider lowering the amount per week, and purchasing from local farms or companies that you know treat their animals with care and compassion. Also, animal farming accounts for high emissions of carbon dioxide and nitrous oxide which are detrimental to the planet. We can't deny the link between animal consumption and climate change.

Here are some ideas on how you can be a more conscious consumer:

- *Consider alternatives to leather-based products (shoes, coats, purses). Companies such as Mat & Nat and Bare Boheme make vegan leather products, or just buy products made from cotton.*

- *Shop at secondhand stores and thrift shops. Re-using clothes cuts down on the amount of trash that ends up in our landfills.*

- *Limit or stop use of plastic bags (storage and shopping bags), plastic utensils and plastic straws. Instead, try reusable canvas shopping bags, reusable silicone storage bags, and bamboo straws. Politely decline plastic bags from store clerks when you buy small items that you can just carry out of the store.*

- *Consider alternatives to wool (sheep fur) products, like cotton.*

- *Shop at stores that care about the Earth and the people. While these clothes may cost more, you might find that you need to buy less clothes the higher the quality they are. Try Patagonia, Amour Vert and Alternative Apparel on for size.*

- *Support restaurants that use organic, local ingredients and ethically sourced animal products.*

- *Speak up. Let grocery stores, companies and restaurants know what you want more of. Write a letter or an email, or ask to speak with a manager.*

- *Take a vegan cooking class or experiment at home by cooking with your friends or family. Go vegan one or two days a week and try these healthy and delicious recipes to get started.*

Papaya Smoothie

A half of a Maradol papaya
1.5 C Coconut water
3 Medjool Dates
½ tsp Turmeric (optional)
1 C Ice

Blend everything together until smooth and enjoy!

Oatmeal with Fruit and Nuts

½ C Steel cut oats
½ C Fruit (cranberries, blueberries, apricots)
1 TBL Maple syrup, or to taste
1 ½ C Almond, oat milk or water
1 TBL Chopped Nuts (almonds, walnuts, pecans)

1. Put oatmeal and liquid into a medium saucepan
on the stove and cook according to package instructions.

2. Add any combination of fresh or dried fruit,
nuts and maple syrup to taste.

Hummus and Vegetable Sandwich

2 slices of bread (your choice)
Vegetables of your choice (Grilled vegetable, sliced tomato, lettuce, cucumbers, roasted red peppers, pickle, avocado etc.)

For hummus: 1 15 oz. can Chickpeas
2 Tbsp Tahini
½ - 1 clove Garlic
¼ cup Olive Oil
¼ tsp Sea Salt
Juice of half a Lemon

1. Combine all hummus ingredients in a food processor until desired consistency.
2. Season with additional salt and lemon to taste.
3. Spread hummus on both sides of toasted bread and layer on vegetables.

54

Hot Chocolate

1½ cups oat or almond milk
½ cup water
1½ Tbsp cocoa powder or carob powder
2 Tbsp maple syrup
1 Tbsp coconut sugar or regular sugar
Dash of vanilla extract or vanilla powder, optional

1. Add all ingredients to a saucepan over medium heat.

2. Whisk to incorporate all ingredients until warm.

Pasta with Pesto Sauce and Roasted Broccoli

Pesto:
2 cups packed basil
⅓ cups walnuts or pine nuts
1 large or 2 small cloves of garlic
1 Tbsp lemon juice
½ tsp sea salt
¼ cup olive oil
1-2 Tbsp water, as needed

1. Combine all the pesto ingredients
into a food processor except olive oil and water.

2. While processing the pesto, stream in the olive oil and then the water
until you reach a desired consistency.

Roasted Broccoli:

1 bunch broccoli, trimmed into florets
2 Tbsp olive oil
2 garlic cloves, sliced
Salt and pepper to taste

1. Set oven to 425 degrees. Arrange broccoli on pan and toss with olive oil, garlic, salt and pepper.

2. Roast for 18-20 minutes

Pasta:

Penne, Spaghetti, Orecchiette, Zucchini Noodles or Carrot Noodles

1. Cook the pasta according to the directions on the box. Be sure to add some salt to the cooking water.

2. Reserve a little cooking water. If you are using the veggie noodles, sauté them in a pan with ½ tablespoon of olive oil.

3. Cook until tender and add salt and pepper to taste.

Once the pasta, pesto and broccoli are complete, combine everything together in a large bowl adding as much pesto you would like. Season with additional salt and pepper.

A New World

We live in a time with overwhelming acts of hate driven by fear, but there have been even greater acts of love, compassion, and kindness. Sometimes it takes people to learn lessons of love through pain, but it doesn't have to happen that way. If we all could stay connected to our source of God and stay in faith that He is guiding us to our greatest good, love will prevail.

Love can heal everything. Miracles flow naturally as long as we stay in faith and love. We are the ones who can change this world. So, do your part, inspire others, and live your best life, the life God intended for you. Don't let anybody or anything get in the way of what you believe to be true. Listen to your heart, for that is God guiding you to your best life.

"Never doubt that a small group of thoughtful, committed citizens can change the world. Indeed, it is the only thing that ever has."
- Margaret Mead

"Somewhere Over The Rainbow / What A Wonderful World"
— Israel Kamakawiwo'ole 18 / 19 / 20

Somewhere over the rainbow
Way up high
And the dreams that you dreamed of
Once in a lullaby

Somewhere over the rainbow
Bluebirds fly
And the dreams that you dreamed of
Dreams really do come true

Someday I'll wish upon a star
Wake up where the clouds are far
Behind me
Where trouble melts like lemon drops
High above the chimney top
That's where you'll find me

Somewhere over the rainbow
Bluebirds fly
And the dream that you dare to,
Oh why, oh why can't I?

Well I see trees of green and red roses too,
I'll watch them bloom for me and you
And I think to myself
What a wonderful world

Well I see skies of blue
And I see clouds of white
And the brightness of day
I like the dark
And I think to myself
What a wonderful world

The colors of the rainbow so pretty in the sky
Are also on the faces of people passing by
I see friends shaking hands
Singing, "How do you do?"
They really sing, "I...I love you"

I hear babies cry and I watch them grow
They'll learn much more than we'll know
And I think to myself
What a wonderful world

Someday I'll wish upon a star
Wake up where the clouds are far
Behind me
Where trouble melts like lemon drops
High above the chimney top
That's where you'll find me

Oh, somewhere over the rainbow
Way up high
And the dream that you dare to
Why, oh why can't I? I?

Epilogue

While the practices written in this book may seem simple, it's no secret that it's not always easy to live by God's will of love and kindness all the time. The best all of us can do is try our best every day, and when we make mistakes, to forgive ourselves, so that we can move on in a better direction. Don't be discouraged, even our perceived "failures" in life are valuable lessons for us to learn from. Whenever you feel in doubt, pray, be kind, and peace will follow.

The following is an excerpt from The Course in Miracles:

"Whenever you are in doubt what you should do, think of His Presence in you, and tell yourself this, and only this:

He leadeth me and knows the way which I know not.
Yet He will never keep from me what He would have me learn.
And so I trust Him to communicate to me all that He knows for me.

Then let Him teach you quietly how to perceive
your guiltlessness, which is already there."
(T-14.III.19:1-5)[21]

Time To Love!

Humans, distracted, busy, fearful, lonely, asleep.

Having forgotten our Purpose, not quite daring to go deep,

We continue to continue, avoiding the Infinite Void that we are.

Avoiding at all costs, Truth memories sleep, our eyes don't see the scar

That keeps us wounded and afraid, forgetting our innate Power.

Forgetting that Life can be so sweet, we lose each moment, each hour.

Not war, nor disaster, nor plague or pandemic has awakened us yet!

In quiet desperation, we are content to be complacent, refusing to reset.

What will it take? What shaking is needed to break the slumber?

What Light is bright enough to shatter the darkness of this blunder?

Will the Light of 1000 Suns be enough? Surely something will work!

A great scientist or philosopher? Where does the answer lurk?

What is missing from the lives that we lead without glee?

Could it be Compassion, or Love or Trust, or all three?

It seems that in all our explorations, we have found

That money cannot replace Love if we want Joy to abound.

Let us shift our focus from our heads to our Hearts,

Allowing our Love to flow in all directions, not just in fits and starts,

But in a continuous flow, a waterfall of Love is what it will take!

How many continuous waterfalls of Love will it take for us to awake?

Without counting, let's each just begin to flow, allow, and emerge.

The more we open, the brighter we become, and the more we merge,

Leaving the experience of separation behind and returning to the state

Of Oneness that was always intended...Yes! That is our Fate!

Suggested Readings

A Return to Love, Marianne Williamson

A Politics of Love, Marianne Williamson

A New Earth, Eckhart Tolle

The Time Is Now: A Call to Uncommon Courage, Joan Chittister

The Universal Christ: How a Forgotten Reality Can Change Everything We See, Hope For, and Believe, Richard Rohr

A Testament of Hope: The Essential Writings and Speeches, Martin Luther King Jr

The Four Agreements, Don Miguel Ruiz

Chloe's Kitchen: 125 Easy, Delicious Recipes for Making the Food You Love the Vegan Way, Chloe Coscarelli

Chloe's Vegan Desserts: More than 100 Exciting New Recipes for Cookies and Pies, Tarts and Cobblers, Cupcakes and Cakes--and More!, Chloe Coscarelli

Online Videos

Prince Harry & Meghan Markle's Wedding Sermon on Love by Bishop Michael Curry

Kanye West's Sunday Service

Joaquin Phoenix's 2020 Oscars Speech

Podcasts

Oprah's Super Soul Conversations

TV Shows

Oprah's Super Soul Sunday on OWN Network

Kim Kardashian West: The Justice Project on Oxygen Network (can be viewed online as well)

Documentary

Bethany Hamilton: Unstoppable

Songs

We Are the World: USA for Africa, Lionel Richie & Michael Jackson

From A Distance, Bette Midler

References

[1] From A Course in Miracles, copyright ©1992, 1999, 2007 by the Foundation for Inner Peace, 448 Ignacio Blvd #306 Novato, CA 94949, www.acim.org and info@acim.org, used with permission. T-1. VII.2:1

[2] Zukav, Gary, Seat of the Soul, pg. 19, Simon & Schuster, (1989).

[3] Reprinted by arrangement with The Heirs to the Estate of Martin Luther King Jr., c/o Writers House as agent for the proprietor New York, NY. © 1963 Dr. Martin Luther King, Jr., copyright © renewed 1991 Coretta Scott King.

[4] Reprinted by arrangement with The Heirs to the Estate of Martin Luther King Jr., c/o Writers House as agent for the proprietor New York, NY. © 1968 Dr. Martin Luther King, Jr., copyright © renewed 1996 Coretta Scott King.

[5] Carroll, May. The Moss and Green, www.themossandgreen.com (last visited February 2,2020).

[6]True Colors
Words and Music by Billy Steinberg and Tom Kelly
Copyright (c) 1986 Sony/ATV Music Publishing LLC
All Rights Administered by Sony/ATV Music Publishing LLC, 424 Church Street, Suite 1200, Nashville,
TN 37219
International Copyright Secured All Rights Reserved
Reprinted by Permission of Hal Leonard LLC

[7] The Four Agreements © 1997 by don Miguel Ruiz and Janet Mills. Reprinted by permission of Amber-Allen Publishing, San Rafael, California. All rights reserved. www.thefouragreements.com.

[8] From A Course in Miracles, copyright ©1992, 1999, 2007 by the Foundation for Inner Peace, 448 Ignacio Blvd #306 Novato, CA 94949, www.acim.org and info@acim.org, and used with permission.

[9] Williamson, Marianne. A Return to Love, (in reference to "A Course in Miracles") page 23, Harper Collins (1992).

[10] A Million Dreams
Words and Music by Benj Pasek and Justin Paul
Copyright (c) 2017 Breathelike Music, Pick In A Pinch Music and T C F Music Publishing, Inc.
All Rights for Breathelike Music and Pick In A Pinch Music Administered Worldwide by Kobalt Songs
Music Publishing
All Rights Reserved Used by Permission
Reprinted by Permission of Hal Leonard LLC

[11] The Peace Flag Project, www.thepeaceflagproject.org
(last visited May 2, 2020).

[12] Bombas, home page, www.bombas.com
(last visited May 2, 2020)

[13] Toms Shoes, home page, www.toms.com
(last visited February 2, 2020)

[14] The Kind Kraft Project, https://www.thekindkraftproject.com/
(last visited June 28, 2020)

[15] FEED, home page, www.feedprojects.com
(last visited May 2, 2020)

[16] Skylar, Giving Back, https://skylar.com/pages/step-up
(last visited May 2, 2020)

[17] TenTree, About Page, https://www.tentree.ca/pages/about (last visited June 3,, 2020)

[18] OVER THE RAINBOW
Music by HAROLD ARLEN
Lyrics by E.Y. HARBURG
Copyright © 1938 (Renewed) METRO-GOLDWYN-MAYER INC.
© 1939 (Renewed) EMI FEIST CATALOG INC.
All Rights Controlled and Administered by EMI FEIST CATALOG INC. (Publishing) and ALFRED MUSIC (Print)
All Rights Reserved
Used By Permission of ALFRED MUSIC
FOR OUR 100% CONTROL - EXCLUDING EUROPE
Fee: $300.00

[19] WHAT A WONDERFUL WORLD
Words and Music by GEORGE DAVID WEISS and BOB THIELE
Copyright © 1967 (Renewed) RANGE ROAD MUSIC INC., BUG MUSIC-QUARTET MUSIC INC. and ABILENE MUSIC, INC. (Administered by IMAGEM MUSIC, LLC)
All Rights for RANGE ROAD MUSIC INC. Controlled and Administered by ROUND HILL CARLIN, LLCAll Rights Reserved
Used By Permission of ALFRED MUSIC
FOR OUR 37.5% CONTROL IN THE WORLD - EXCLUDING EUROPE
FOR OUR 50% CONTROL IN EUROPE
Fee: $112.50

[20] What A Wonderful World
Words and Music by George David Weiss and Bob Thiele
Copyright (c) 1967 by Range Road Music Inc., Quartet Music and Abilene Music
Copyright Renewed
All Rights for Range Road Music Inc. Administered by Round Hill Carlin, LLC
All Rights for Quartet Music Administered by BMG Rights Management (US) LLC

68

[21] From A Course in Miracles, copyright ©1992, 1999, 2007 by
the Foundation for Inner Peace, 448 Ignacio Blvd #306 Novato, CA
94949, www.acim.org and info@acim.org, used with permission. (T-
14.III.19:1-5)

Made in the USA
Middletown, DE
11 December 2020